THE GOING-UNDER OF THE EVENING-LAND

AND

OTHER POEMS

BY DAVID CHURCHILL

THE GOING-UNDER OF THE EVENING-LAND
AND OTHER POEMS

© 2013 David Churchill

Cover art courtesy of Ivor Matanle
Graphic by Alexis Millan
Book layout by Barbara Shaw

Third Edition

Published by:
Pony One Dog Press
PO Box 30552
Bethesda, Maryland 20824

To those who were there . . .

Contents

OTHER POEMS

Bishop Asbury on Horseback
16th & Mount Pleasant Streets

It is June and the grass is high:
no one has mowed
this pasture yet—
Still the Bishop plods on,
oblivious to the sun;
where he is
it's been raining for days.

Old Revelator droops his head,
footsore and weary,
but the man on his back
is not tired: he rides
with one finger
tucked in his book,
a few crumbs of johnny-cake
all the sustenance he needs.

From the front you see
the past night in the cabin
at the foot of the tree-cliff,
where he knelt with the parents
whose child had been called
beyond the crest of a hill;

men have their feet
in the earth at all times
in this country;
in front of its mystery

they can only kneel
in order to get closer to it—
but there were too many
for the Bishop to stay long . . .

Only the old men
on the benches behind him,
easing their bones,
see the spires before him.

The Return
Washington DC 2010

His feet were a breeze
of many directions.
They wafted him down the street,
wagging at every pair
of knees in his path,
eyes full of hope;
what city this was,
I don't even know—

he was a dog
with his ribs for a home . . .
Next we were
surrounded by sampans,
colorful corals
whitening on the driveway;
the year after that,
elsewhere again . . .

But you have to pick some
place to return to:
the year *I* returned,
things were the same,
yet different—
sidewalks were crowded
with people who hadn't
been born,
last time I was here—

An old man passed . . .
overcoats on
like the ages of a life,
blind to the magic
of seeing the past
still alive—
In his face I saw a choice:
an open door
and a gust of wind,
a house full of ghosts.

Boardwalk
Ocean City, MD 2005

Hello, my name is Elga.
My home is in Finland.
Following what your training
recommends me to do,
is proceeding better than I dreamed.
Please buy a drink from me.

Hello, I'm Mani. Are you
desperate from your country?
I came five thousand miles
to wear a cone on my head.
Please buy some ice cream.

Hello, I'm Bridget.
Tired of being embarrassed on bed?
I work twelve-hour shifts.
We sleep ten in a room.
I will go home soon
with a hole in my tooth.

Live
Christmas, 2004

Some offer him popcorn,
others toys made by children;
I offer mad hatters
and bellhops, glittering
and colorful,
from a warehouse of dreams.

Some offer him orbs,
string lights in his nebulae,
red yellow blue,
all lengths of the spectrum;
others prefer white,
what they can see.

Some give him garlands,
others give tinsel,
sparkling and silvery;
others hang icicles
as if it were snowing.

Make ready my place.
Bear me in on your backs.
Pour me libations.
I fill your home with the blessings of balsam.
Bring me your tribute.

Bedside
2/6/1977

The tape was transparent—
if her eyelids had opened
she could have looked through it . . .

but they didn't,
at least not while I stood there.
Now in my mind
I stand there again,
looking at a woman
whose eyes are taped shut,

their vision still burning
like a negative light
whose shadows are the only things you see . . .

Though perhaps not for *us*—
but for the sky,
for ice and Navaho stone,
for veins of azurite,
for all colors of blue,
perhaps above all for all eyes—
for eyes as blue as a coal-miner's eyes . . .

I stand here now weighed down.
Some words,
like certain eyes,
though gone,
cannot be closed.

Forgive what I said—
as you forgave those tubes
that breathed for you,
entirely inward
in the twilit room,
not hearing
the whisper of shoes,
or the bleat of machines
that finally devoured you.

Forgive my small weight,
unable to support you.

Silence will fall
in a dry kingdom,
and your heart
will grow loud in the silence.

The Triumph of Everyday Living
Germantown, Maryland

The signal awakes,
caught off-guard;
the rails tense.
A river of mercury
pours into space.

You find a seat,
settle into your paper.
You've done this so often,
you no longer see
the faces around you—
and no one sees you.

Not for the young
is this, nor for those
who rearrange every day—
For them every day
is the new
and their pulse is its engine.

This is for you
who have the power
of mountains,
who like the mountains
are here every day,

who look out a window
sometimes

and can't remember
the time,
or which direction you're going—
and know it doesn't matter.

D. M.

To the immortal shades of a dune
on the Mediterranean shore,
with the air for walls and rafters of stars—
to the shades of the souls
of the boys who were there—
libertus sibi posterisque suis,
"a freedman, for himself and his descendants,"
to the shades of the coals of the fire,
bene merens . . . .

To the shades of a café in Turkey
in a village somewhere on a dusty plateau,
with sheep heads on tables and glasses of tea—
to the shades of the silence
of the boys who were there—
vixit annos XC menses X diebus XXVI,
"ninety years, ten months, twenty-six days,"
to the shades of a secret—
bene merens . . .

To the shades of a house newly stilled,
the equipment in the bedroom,
newly stilled—to a long story told
by the last of many wives,
how he brushed her lips lightly
with a secretive kiss,
in ignem inlatus est,
you die when the last person

who remembers you dies—
bene merens . . .
"well-deserving . . . "

Boardwalk
Ocean City, Maryland 2010

I

Where is everyone going?
The answer is nowhere:
they have already arrived.
It is the end of the day,
nothing left but pure motion.

II

Screams fill the air—
Caterpillars are carrying
kids on their backs;
hippos don't care,
flying in loopy pairs.
No space between—?
Children are flung
from ride to ride.
Candy-colors swirl and dive.

III

Come—join the parade.
Zebra-heads and
shaved squirrels are on display.
Gulls swarm a crumb
as burn-jockeys pass,
red as fire-plugs.
Henna-punks materialize,
their eyes the first places
the sun disappears from.

IV

Grab fist-fulls of jewelry,
fling in the back of a closet,
plug them in—:
a pulsating bangle
around a gigantic arm,
a cyclone of lights,
scenes of destruction—
Take a flying-carpet ride,
or just feel giddy standing still.
The whole night
tilt-wheels around you.

V

Listen, someone is singing.
Can you hear him—?
A song flings its veil
across the throats of the crowd.
A guitar-case is open,
a coffin for change.

Autumn

Michigan Ave, Washington DC

Perhaps it was the clouds—
the source of light
no longer behind them
but beneath them,
coming from the duskred leaves

and gold leaves,
that made jellybeans float
from an open-house sign,
and a cluster escaped
and tangled in a telephone line

among the terrestrial ambers,
pewter shadows
and colorful flannels—
and always the reds,
grayreds and monarch reds,
that someone had staged . . .

At the end of the block,
a trinity of shades,
redblack bluegreen
and marigold,
controlled everything around them,
approving the scheme.

Katrina
8/29/2010

After the wind stopped blowing,
a second wind blew.
No one could feel it—
It blew the people away.

Ten days we rode,
we didn't know where.
We slept most of the time.
No one could tell us anything.

We in a new home now.
Set everything out to dry in the sun.
Doyle, he moved on—
He in Kansas somewhere,
got a new family there.

Five years gone by—
still I see those two dogs,
Bandit and Pooch.
They knew they weren't coming.
I tell my baby shut up—
We left them on the roof.

Fountains in Rain
Washington DC April 2009

Siege-ladders raise against clouds;
drains overflow,
streams of monuments
are cleaned
that pour into bowls.
The time to look at fountains is in the rain.

Everyone is gone and I'm alone .
Only the figures
at the bases of fountains
are left: they'd like
to run too but can't—
fountains don't turn off:

Some with cupped palms
let water pour,
others dance naked;
still more simply
weep for joy
out of wide-opened eyes—

For those who walk
alone in the rain,
fountains come into their own.

[39]

To be dead is to be bones
for someone to bury—
To be more than dead
is to be less than the air itself
that people look through,
when they seem to look at you
but see nothing.
Thus living do you walk
through the shades of the evening,
and know freedom,
for the dead at least can still
claim a memory,
but nothing calls you its own.

Who is the one whose eyes
will be the beautiful
doors to this void?
You will pass through
as one passes into a pool
where not even your own reflection
rises to meet you
and no surface sounds
as you knock,
and you are released
like a moth in a world without sun.

Perhaps because the living
are already ghosts to you . . .
Less than the reflections
of air in a mirror,
they are invisible to you;
you have not yet given them
the power to hold you.
You alone desire others
as one desires a soul.

Here raise a few sticks
to make a roof
under the brow of a low hill,
and the smoke of your fire
will be beyond alone in the sky;
here dwell entirely alone—
until like an invalid
every memory of health
will have passed,
and a child will appear,
to lead you again
to those who merely live,
who have chosen you.

Big-Dog Walk
Great Seneca Greenway Trail

The transformation begins
with a blade of green grass.
After that it's a mystery
as to what happens next.

His ears become voles,
arresting him in his tracks;
his nose becomes a fox,
pulling him in circles—

His legs become deer,
racing to a place
that will only be known
when everyone gets there.

When his tongue
becomes the stream,
birds fly to their twigs
and a moccasin glides
across the trail and disappears . . .

Always the Young Strangers

When you write
poetry,
do only this:
believe in one line.

For every meaning
linked,
another undone.

Their words
are as light
through trees;
their belief
is in moss
and the flattery of weeds.

Deer move through
woods
without roads.

Cherry Bend Drive
2009

1

This window once
framed a pink thundercloud;
now the cloud is green.
Inside, the cold of eventual
autumns makes the collie sleep,
the cat lies in a circle of sun.
Children's voices have receded,
drawing down their waves
in this country without a city.

Like a shell against the ear,
the house still murmurs
with its years, reminding us
its walls still hold
the flotsam of our lives:
tempest winds,
Laestrygonian landscapes,
whirlpools and seascapes—

Or was it I who refused
stick-figure houses,
uncomfortable with rainbows
and the outline of daisies?

Too long I have been under
the sign of the crab.

I have had trouble with people
who are ruled by the moon.
I have been warned
to avoid moonlight on rain water,
to be aware around pools
and in any kind of tide.

Now at this window I stare out—
and I see that the leaves
that all summer have burned
are tired of being green,
and will soon be consumed.

The sap will return to the root,
to warm in the earth,
to fill again with green,
draw shade out of the ground,
soak up new breezes,
new air and light,
everything that can burn
from the full earth,
for a world that will have forgotten.

What will I tell them,
those sailors of summer,
when rainclouds of blossoms
darken *their* windows,
and summer will be gone?

2

Bells ring and a steam-cloud
announces the bellow of a horn,
short—short—long——
crying its hurt across the water.
The throbbing ceases
and the ship becomes silent.
Adults shift impatiently
and children feel annoyed
in their torsos of kapok,
looking like trolls—

A life-boat bangs against the glass,
testing the air
at the end of its davits . . .
then is withdrawn.
Beyond the scrim of salt-encrusted panes,
a star-filled canton
flutters horizontally.
Thus was our routine
of danger avoided,
and we returned to our play . . .

or to stand at the stern
hanging over the rail,
watching old faces form
in the boil of the wake

and sink again drowned,
and new faces seethe up
and become clouds.

On the oceans it's like this:
distance is measured in faces.

3

This is what I will tell them:
that it was on a day like today,
when leaves were greenblack and limp,
that a young man arose,
and while the world slept,
walked to a road
where a storm-cloud was forming,
and set out to find them.

Haiku: Snowfall in Autumn

A curtain comes down
on a circus of leaves—
and keeps coming down,
unable to close
on this colorful show.

The Year I Didn't Go to School
in Ankara, Turkey

Always the sky would be a dome
with the sun on the inside
as I walked down the hill,
taking a back road,
hearing the muezzin's call
broadcast over the valley,
and a donkey bray—

until my feet touched earth again.
Then the nests of storks
on their chimneys,
empty since autumn,
would be dusted with snow,
and workmen in waistcoats
shoveled cement
up the sides of slow buildings.

Behind me in the Twenty-Third of May
the house would be cold,
only Mom still asleep.
Soon Mehmet would arrive
to stoke the furnace,
shovel a little coal,
a man with two wives,
an old one in the country,
a new one in the city.

A hundred hours staring
at tea urns and tambourines—
eighty hours in doorways—
twenty hours on a bench
in Youth Park—
ten hours in a train-station—

an hour more waiting
for the sun to go down . . .

Walking out on the Beach after Dark
Bethany Beach, July, 2011

Our feet make no sound
as we walk across the dunes;
the sand tugs at our legs
as though it would still motion too,
until we reach the tide—
but even there the night gives back
no scrape of step,
though it is an echo chamber
for the heartbeat of the sea . . .

for a moment, the only thing
that lets you know it's there—
Without anything to see,
the dark closes in, though you know
no walls surround you.
Behind us on the boardwalk
people look out
on their shadows on the sand;

I would tell them, go back,
forget the ocean after dark,
there's nothing here.
But still they come, like us,
looking for something . . .
Suddenly a mug runs over
and we're standing in foam,
the only thing that sparkles . . .
other than our eyes.

How cold the water is!
Too late to remove shoes—
The dark claims its own.
At least for the dead
the sea will be warm.

In Care of Bodies
Ocean City, Maryland, 2010

The ocean is like a lake.
No wind—the lazy
thunder of surf breaks
over the tabernacles
in invisible waves.

Every age of body
is here on the beach:
today they are like candles
with a single flame,
though time is the heat
that will melt this wax.

Sinners burn in hell
across a nearby trapezius,
bleeding down an arm
into a colorful sleeve;
this man is never naked:
he likes his clothes
right on his skin—

but the rest are disrobed
or nearly so,
some tied in string
as though their bodies
would explode,
others with curtains

on their limbs
as though the sea was a shower.

Does it matter
if one limb is stout
and the other is lean?
In this glare
all eyes are hidden:
the whole air is a mirror,
bright as a scalpel.

An aphrodite appears,
wandering among the towels.
I see sand
on her legs,
a cloud across the sun.

MÜNCHEN

1

There, at the border of the field—
there, on the river-bank,
there, overlooking a white beach—
flat troll head peering over the brows of earth,
cyclopean eye able to comprise whole horizons
in a single stare—

Infecting with silence the fields they guard,
these concrete forms still stand
where defenders constructed them,
full of the purpose of safety.
Only the wind breaks their silence
and now and then a disturbance
of children, more attuned to war
than to peace,
who would play on a guillotine
if you let them.

Follow the path through the woods
to the edge of the field—
There something lives in hidden places,
old concrete turning to cave,
known now only to children.
It sets your heart leaping.
You approach alone or with a friend—
It is a secret you share:

anything could happen there,
a left-over excitement that still could explode.

I learned about love from places like these.
I learned anatomy from the walls of pill-boxes.
I learned how to make love to a woman
from the drawings on walls.
I learned positions from abandoned fortifications.

What was war like? Let me tell you.
My Hans was in Poland in thirty-nine.
Everyone loved a winner then—
The men were hard all the time.
As for the Jewish girls,
well, one had power over them.
Of course, after Stalingrad,
no one could get it up . . .

Under a low ceiling,
in the half-light of gun-slits,
the floor covered with shit
and the excitement of flies,
I studied the drawings on the walls
and inhaled the odor
and thought I also knew
what a world without rules was like.

That day Margarethe
took us for a walk along the riverbank,
skipped stones with us,
explained the logic of a bridge
with two decks,
where the trains crossed with their banners of smoke,
how if the Allies bombed the top,
the bottom could be used,
and the other ways they outsmarted us.

My life has not turned out as I expected.
How can I explain?
I trained to be a teacher in the occupied lands,
teaching German to the children
of subjugated Poles—
It seems there were two of me then,
a woman who dreamed
and a woman who worked;
in the beginning the woman who dreamed was alive,
later it was the other, the woman who worked;
now I can see
I was never really either,
neither dreaming nor working,
but a shadow of something else—
Now I run the lift at the Adler Hotel,
go to my room reeking

of cigars, the perfume of cheap women.
I remember often the lindens of my youth,
planted so firmly in orderly rows:
each year the blossoms were too early or too late.
Why did I not see
this was where History had assigned me?

The Move
2011

He says this goes, this stays.
He lifts whole houses
on his back,
clears rooms with one arm.

She sees the smile of a child,
a head bowed over homework,
how like the dust
on a butterfly wing,
the temperature of air in the spring.

State Fair
Timonium, Maryland 2010

The crowd is like clouds,
pressing together—
till lightening appears.
But this lightening can be ridden,
will guess your weight
or tell you your age,
test your aim
and hand you a prize.

We head straight for the animals.
A whirring of fans
fills the shed.
The air is odorous and close:
you feel your pulse slow.
It could rain buckets
and you would be
comfortable and safe.

The work of chewing
progresses apace . . .
Sheep speak their
single-word language.
People reach out,
try to touch, caress, take
to themselves
from the oblivious forms,
sunk like boulders
in the holiday of hay.

A cow ambles by,
reduced to essentials,
pin-bones and milk veins,
led by a child—
I look at the farm-folk,
sitting in circles;
they take it in stride.
A teen-ager sleeps,
his cheek like a peach.

Lifeguard in Rain

Ocean City, Maryland, 2010

Is it the law that requires
you to man your watchtower
in primordial gray,
when the bounds of the world
have been loosed
and the sea fills the sky?

Out of the fogbank in front of you
white streamers flatten
and race to your feet—
What message do they bring,
that nothing is before you
but fog and waves?
And the rain
beats down the sandcastles.

Or the lone figure
who appears on the beach?
Is it for him that you watch,
who feels his skin
plucked by the rain—
afraid of the sea
that wears a more honest look,
as if it really weren't meant
to be bathed in at all;
he wades in the surf,
then picks up a beach-toy
and goes on,
still looking for something . . . ?

July Fourth, 2010
Roof of the Kennedy Center, Washington, DC

Last year's embers still burn,
silver, red, gold,
scattered over the shores
where they fell as the last echoes
died over the hills,

giving up violence
and resigned to live in peace.
Suddenly the first
salvo is fired—
the bombardment
of Fort McHenry

is happening again.
We share what
the first defenders experienced:
fire-sperms lash
up the sky and disappear—
a final shock
unlocks the heart.
Around the horizon
umbrellas of fire are raised.

A billion light-years away
an astronomer
watches the birth of a universe.
We leave feeling
we know what he's seen.

Fox, Dawson Farm Road

All winter he lay there,
and the winter was good to him.
The wind stroked him
and the snow wove a blanket
and the cold told him
he could stay there forever.

But summer betrayed him.
The warm rain dissolved him,
his tail abandoned him,
his teeth bared to the sun;
the mowers mowed around him
and the grass made him a tomb—

All summer long
the birds sang him their song:
"Take up and read!"
"Take up and read!"
But their song fell on ears
already listening to the ground—

The sun finally forgot him
and the mowers forgot him
and the wind forgot him
and the rain forgot him
and the birds sing their songs
for other ears now—

But there is always that place
where the grass is a little greener.
The dog always stops there
and I stop there too,
slacking the leash.

The Girl in the Next Lane

Water smooth as silk—
until she dives,
then a thousand ripples
flee to every corner of the pool:

before they return
she has lapped them already.
Under the surface
she is an eel in lycra;

her own fan-club of bubbles
can barely keep up.
The water is fast today
and soon I'm breathing hard:

wall, somersault,
a flash of white legs beside me,
then the long stripe
of the bottom, leading to deep water.

For whole laps
we keep pace, stroke for stroke,
her body mirroring mine;
the water between us
as clear as a lens.

When I drive home
I am thinking of nothing.

All around us sleek cars
are at rest, nobody moving.
The air is opaque,
difficult to breathe.

Cosmo

Many have praised
Dante's visions of heaven:
his gold mirror in the sun,
his white rose . . .
But Dante never saw
a white cat with blue eyes.

Take an azure sky with white clouds,
turn it inside-out,
add whiskers,
the pink of future dawns
in nose and ears,
the cold gaze of an angel of prey,

and you will have made a cherub
the old-fashioned way.
But I am not thinking
of theological things:
I am watching a cat
fishing for water
in the bowl of a toilet
with a paw like a cauliflower—

He is the world,
and the world is real.
He is my familiar,
though I don't know how to use him yet.

[16]

Now I know
I could live without a head:
I forgot to set the alarm
but my body got up anyway.

My body could find
its own way to work:
one day I awoke
and had driven the whole way
and hadn't hit a thing—

Sometimes my body
goes in a room
and then stops,
and I wonder—
What is it looking for?
I hope it's not looking for me.

Water on Water
Storm at Ocean City, Maryland, 2008

The children have given up
throwing sand at the waves
and grandparents
have given up giving names to the waves

and those who didn't need to be saved
have been saved,
and those who did
have been burnt to Hiroshimas

and the life-girl has pulled
her chair back
and the umbrella-guy
has removed the umbrellas
and the gulls
have taken their wind-bodies home,

and a last bather
trudges over the dunes.
No sign is put up
but this beach is closed.

The sky dips wet paper
in a stencil of the distance,
soaks up blues, greens . . .
a vein throbs
in the cloud—

Rip the paper in two,
put it back sideways . . .
Now it's raining.

Requiem

It wasn't when I carried him in
and you took us straight back
past the yapping and sniffing
and puddles of the waiting room,
to a special room in the back,

and it wasn't the carpet
on the floor or the pictures
of forest trails on the walls,

and it wasn't when he got up
and decided to walk again,
and got out the door
and almost dragged himself to freedom,

and it wasn't when you said
it was the hardest part
of your job and you sat
on the floor and cradled his head,

it was when you asked me
how long we'd had him.

We got him as an adult.
He was a rescue dog.
He wasn't house-broken
and he had other problem behaviors,
but he tried to be a good boy
and he had a good life.

Thank you for letting me tell you.

Avernus

Etruscan Tombs, Cerveteri 1952

Cooperation was what it took
to rob these tombs:
someone to tramp
the growth that protected their sleep,
or at least the sleep
of the archeologists
who robbed them first—

and someone to crawl
into the cool dark,
someone who could fit
under a low lintel
or over blocked rubble—

Not much room to stand up
but plenty to lie down in
on the shelves along the walls
if you wanted to nap;
these were middle-class tombs,
no wall-paintings here,

but pottery a-plenty,
remnants of funeral meals,
and in one: a *bucchero* cup,
black-fired pottery,
a chink out of the lip
where someone drank too deep.

Where are they now, those treasures—
those shards we
carried home so proudly,
rich in designs,
to decorate a bookcase . . .

where is that cup
a bearded man raised
to celebrate the dead,
or to drink to the future?

Ostia Antica, Rome 1953

Here where this memory is,
it's always underground:
it's dark but somehow we see;
the ground wet
like a cave floor,
the dead on the surface
under tented stones.

More dead inside:
sarcophagoi
carved with swags,
putti in carnal stone,
inscriptions chipped away,
faces unformed or
vandalized, hide them.

It took strong arms
to move these lids,
reveal their dust,
what the dead are made of:
baker, fuller, provisioner
of grain,
heap of mingled bones
unable to be parsed.

Here was the right role for a guide:
uncover the eyes,
strengthen the will,
bid us not be afraid,
instill discipline—
forbid us a skull,
allow only an incisor or two.

Necropolis at Pamukkale, Turkey 1960

Did they come here
to take the water before dying?
It is a short distance—
I would rather die cold
and alone than
leave pleasure and comfort
to dry in the earth.

Dusk has stilled the voices of the bathers.
The secretarial pool
is bathing there too.
The sun is going down
and the swifts are imitating
the souls of the dead.

Do all come to twilight then,
who take the water—
seeing yet not seeing,
knowing yet not knowing,
a long lie of living?

These habitations
return to their evening,
sink in their dirt
and planks, the spade
of an archeologist
abandoned in a trench;
homes without doors,
nothing to think about,
nothing to see,
wholly unsatisfactory . . .

Wedding on a Wind-Swept Beach
for David and Melissa
10/19/2008

Everything was there,
though only the people were visible:
the flying-buttresses existed
on an invisible plane.

A surfer cut a wave
behind the gowns and bouquets;
the wedding-gown blew
like the breast of a gull.

More than two families
are gathered today,
but no one need hide:
today everyone hears
the wind,
feels the pull of the tides,

today all is forgiven.
I raise my eyes
to the bride and the bridegroom,
to see if anything on a beach
could anchor the sea,
and hear this poem:

"Life is a journey,
its end is in another—"

and I am satisfied,
for though the earth move,
there is enough here
to build on.

Notes for a Cure
Wednesday Night Group

A black stone, a cactus,
a bowl of candy,
tissues . . .
these are the objects
on the table before you.

Hung on the walls
are images of countrysides:
where would you like
to go today—
that farm in New Hampshire,
the isle of Capri?

The only discordant note
is struck by the clocks:
a clock in a bell-jar,
a music-box clock—
A Cheshire-cat watches with
tick-tocking eyes.

Five floors down
life seems to go on—
Sometimes it snows.
People know where they're going.

The only parking you can find
is ten blocks away . . .

but it doesn't matter.
It's a pleasure to walk.
My people were people
who walked across continents.
Ten centuries of wind
blow against me.

Reading

This, this is the Knave of Coins:
the vending machine will steal your change.
And this, this is the Hanged Man:
the meaning of this is
you will spill food on your tie.

This, this is the Fool,
he is walking off a cliff;
the meaning of this is you will hit a pedestrian.
And this, this is a bad sign,
lightening striking a tower—
Today it simply means
you should have spent more time on your hair.

This, this is your card:
the Man with a Lantern.
The meaning of this
is you are a seeker of the truth.

And this—this is something
no one can show you.
This is someone who is looking
for you on the internet . . .

Girl Cutting Roses
for W.S.Merwin

The scissors make their clean
snap across the stem
and a rose comes free,
leaving one
dew drop on a blade.

These don't belong here
in this plot alone,
no one to see
their curling flame,
white and peach;
how their petal-feathers
puff with pride,
having touched the dawn,

but within, in
water that enlarges thorns,
they will teach
their courage to a cheek,
and while they last,
themselves will be
their own earth.

One Minute
for Margaret Hunter Pierce
6/30/1910 – 3/17/2007

Even in death
she confounded her critics,
remaining unclaimed
because no one
could agree what had killed her,

until in the end
they settled on
the word *old*, and let it go at that.

How she had fit
in the palm of a hand,
how she had been fed
with an eye-dropper,
how her mother
didn't want her
and her father had said
she would never be right,
how she had confounded them all—

until in the end
she confounded even herself,
and all that was left
were the memories
and a few fading stories.

It took a day
to consign them to oblivion,

a minute
in the middle of the night
to write down these words—
If I could have held a pen
I would have written them
in my sleep,
and forgotten in the morning.

Amazing Grace
Atlantic City, New Jersey, December, 1993

Did I tell you—?
A woman played a keyboard
on the boardwalk
at Atlantic City.

She had no arms or legs.
Her tongue was
a pink serpent
that slid from her head,
licking glad notes
into the cold,
gull squealing air.

And it *was* cold—
The wind found few niches
to hide in, few
corners to shelter you,
no one to
toss coins in her bucket.

Yet still she played on,
her song falling
on shuttered arcades,
stilled rides,
the world closed like ears,
no one to hear

except us . . .
and we had heard enough
of this siren of
the money-coast—
We turned up our collars,
hurrying past
tour-buses
unloading their crews.

Haiku
Winter Landscape with Crow

White snow-world,
low still boughs,
black bird knocking
snow down.

Cry, crow,
loud and long.
Your home is in the air,
your food is on
the ground.

Renew

Exercise is only good for one day.
One walk is not enough
for the dog.
Why won't the dishes
stay out of the dishwasher—
where is the thing
that is only done once?

A wheel rises in the dark:
the windows of the car
are lidded in frost—
It is morning again,
the paper knocks at the door.

I stand again before the mirror,
built like a closet
with doors on its sides:
while I shave,
infinite echoes arise
of my hands,
throwing stones into infinite
ponds.

Ours is an eternity
broken into pieces—
the rest is illusion.

The only other things
are ancestors in uniform
—or clothes that resemble them—
marching out of the walls.

Somewhere an owl blinks
and it is dark again.
I am home under stars
that haven't moved since November.
I close the car door
and look up,
beyond the elements of Orion—

There is a mismatch
between things.
I can almost see it
in the space between stars.

Letter to Amanda
to Amanda in Utah

Rock walls rise high
around you. The wind
rages down canyons.
Water created these cliffs.
It took awhile.

We lied to get you here.
Lies closed us in.
It was how we lived.
We used to drop you
at school; the not-
knowing was hard.
The silence destroyed us.

Now the cottonwood
greens. The wind
sings in the canyons.
You write of a foal
that was born in the field.
Bob pulled it
from its mother; a normal
birth in that place.

We will visit you soon.
We will walk by
the river where it flows
from the rock.

We will climb
to a high pool,
arrive panting, out of breath.
You will show us
the new foal,
far away,
running with its mother.

Working Late

Seven pm—the guard nods
as you leave: at this hour
he's everyone's friend.
It's dark already,
the parking-lot empty—
the whole world's departed.

The boss ordered pizza.
It was almost a party:
everyone bonded.
While the building slowly stilled
we stayed at our posts,
steering our enterprise
into uncharted waters.
The car is your lifeboat.

Traffic's lighter—that's good,
you'll get home sooner;
you think of that one bright house
at the edge of the continent,
lit like an ember;
already there in mind,
you look in through the window,
see children at a table,
the outline of a woman . . .

When you arrive, everything's dark.
The cats have been fed,

the dog walked,
the children in their beds—
One light still shines:
"I took the trash out . . . "
As you slide into bed
you feel for her foot,
brush your sole across her heel,
across the arch
of her instep.

March, 2006

If we could see wind,
what would it look like?
Would it be air-dogs
chasing down the street,
knocking over trash-cans,
scattering the trash?

Or would it be ponies
galloping through trees
with mile-long manes
and nostrils like wind-tunnels,
eddying in backyard corrals,
knocking against wind-chimes?

And when hurricanes come—
would it be like buffalo
covering the sky,
pursued by clouds
in the shape of war bonnets,
toward some cliff
at the edge of creation?

Bryce Canyon National Park
Farview Point, May, 2005

This is not what I like:
eyes stretched
from compass-point to compass-point,
ninety degrees of blue
in one glance;
below, thousand-foot cliffs
only eagles can see—
One might as well be blind.

The landforms of three states
approach to be sheltered,
while the spires and buttresses
that preceded them
ignite at our feet
as they raise themselves up,
entering the escarpment.

Give me a junk shop,
full of things to sink your eyes in:
door-knobs and keys
that have opened
enough doors for the hands
that once touched them
to follow into oblivion—

At least let me go back
to the souvenir shop;
I am not fit for grand views.

Let me hide
among shelves of small things,
the feet of the rabbit,
the eyes of a stuffed fox—
where I can relax
with unnecessary purchases.

Spring in Six Days
Cherry Bend Drive, Germantown

Day one birds
in the dark,
raising a racket.

Day two trees
are hot,
pink and white popcorn.

Day three a
cold rain;
blossoms on ice.

Day four first
green,
pagodas in trees.

Day five confetti
on cars,
party in progress.

Day six spring is over;
it's ninety degrees.

Rome
1953-1957

Foreign city, under
the heat of a summer noon,
when even the shadow
of a wall gives no relief,
you were my friend.

City, you accompanied me:
you were my map
as I navigated alleys,
conquered vacant lots,
wandered in your markets
buying fish for cats.

Into me like wine
you poured yourself
until, filled with streetcar sparks,
the gravel of walks,
the smell of alabaster
and marble dust,
a far blue haze,
distant as a hush,
lifted me
above your chimney-tops.

City, I was free in you.
I spent whole days in you.
I could have lived
like a cat

had someone fed me;
the only danger was getting lost,
and that was safe.

But in my sleep
you held me,
confusing your streets,
not letting me go,
till finally—home,
finding everything changed,
stairwell floating,
landings hanging,
echoes out of synch—
apartment empty
or strangers there . . .

City, take me back again.
Don't leave me like
a jealous flame.
This home and I
are only friends.

Appalachian Spring

Spruce Knob, West Virginia, 2009

I have been to the top of the world.
I can tell you what's there:
enough flagstones to pave
the bottom of the world,
if anyone cared.

All day the wind combs
red spruce into twisted places,
sighs over mountain laurel
and mountain ash,
adopting the patience of lichen.

We started in summer
and drove up through oaks,
watched leaves drop
dry sunfalls across us,
and arrived in December.

To anyone who asks
I would say this:
go to any summit
and build there a tower,
climb to its top
and reach for a peregrine.

Smoke Hole, West Virginia 2009

If land could sleep
and waking,
watch its own dream fade,
this would be Smoke Hole.

Morning: two flakes
detach from dark flanks,
soar up and combust.
The gorge lifts an eyelid.

Smoke of moonshiners
feeding their still,
Indians curing trout
in the folds of the hills,
drifts up, evaporates . . .

Blackwater Falls, West Virginia 2009
  after ten days of rain

I believe in giants.
I have seen the earth
tilted by a giant,
I have seen water
poured out like a bowl.

You first hear a roar,
see mist flying
out of a gorge.
If water could burn,
this would be smoke.

For one thing this
water's not black:
it is the color of rust.
At the base of the falls
it explodes.

Everything shakes.
The bushes blow back.
The boughs of the hemlocks
quake.

One climbs two
hundred and
fourteen steps to escape.

[13]

If I were a sultan
I'd buy a new wife
for my harem every week
and sire thousands of children
and every now and then
with a wave of a hand
I'd give a girl leave
to go and marry her lover—

If I were rich and unmarried
I'd pursue any number
of skirts—and if married,
I'd wine them by moonlight:
they say when a man's
cornstalk declines,
he needs more honeysuckle vine.

I stood on a corner
and looked into the souls
of old men and the hearts
of old women
and I saw the candles
of youth going out,
like flames without air.

So I will describe you exactly
to a carpenter
who will carve you in wood,

and I will tell a painter
about you
and he will capture
the color in your cheeks,

and I will mount you
on the bow of a ship
and sail for the shore
where giant faces stand,
guarding against marauders
that no longer come.

THE GOING-UNDER OF THE EVENING-LAND

Trees are in bloom all around—pink and white blossoms predominate. And all the green leaves are coming out. We have such lovely poplar trees in back of our house—in a row, and our kitchen window looks out across to the park—a very pretty view. I think springtime in Germany is going to be a very lovely time—.

– Journal Entry, April 17th 1950

I remember looking out our front windows (apartment at Wolfgangstrasse 30) at the bombed buildings—ruins from the war just across the street—and still uncleaned-up and un-rebuilt after 5 years . . . What do I best remember about Frankfurt am Main—now, 15 years later? The bombed and ruined buildings, so much of the city lying in rubble all over in residential areas and in the down-town business districts . . . .

– Postscript, July 20ᵗʰ, 1965

Part One

Prologue

A man on an island had a vision.
He sat on the shore and saw everything clearly:
the sea was the color of baby-blue eyes,
and the sky could be so many things—
mostly an ocean of glitter-points,
especially at noon when the sun
was overhead; the eyes on the boats
in the cove seemed to wink,

taunting him with the possibility
of crossing the straight, an exile of visions,
and the mainland so near, almost
a vision itself, beyond the blue sea-line,
invisible in the distance.
There, people burned with beautiful flames,
and some spoke a language
every man could understand
though no one else spoke it,

and some had the breeze about them
twenty-four hours,
rustling the beads in the doorways,
and some walked every moment
at the edge of the world and never fell off,
or could be seen standing
on air in the dusk of their chambers,
all courteous strangers,
eager to share their crust—

While he, here, alone, had only this:
the dolphin-eyed boats mocking his gaze,
the wine bad, the men untalkative,
the women suspicious
of his tale of a god who killed his son;
and the lonely raptures in the dark,
the wind playing its reed to the pines,
Diana overshining the stars,
flying away from his overfull heart—

In the fire of a candle
the image of a centurion appeared,
a well-mannered youth,
the beard barely out on his chin,
not one of their faith,
yet who took him under his arm,
laid his bed next to his
lest the sailors despoil him,
and who only said once
with a touch of bemusement:
"Is it true what they say,
this savior of yours
was the illegitimate son of a soldier of Rome . . . ?"

Cool, rational hours of the night . . .
with a youth's face in the flame,
holding the shadows at bay—
free from the heat of the sun
that sets glories afoot in the eye-beams:
a pair of baked eyes on the shore,
straining to see beyond the sea-line,

bleeding into the glare,
watching a turtle egg swell . . .

. . . until a boy ripped it open, found
a grown turtle inside, dead—
smothered in its own birth,
a shell that would not crack,
a sign that was spoken of in the village;
to him, full of sadness . . .

To some was given the past,
to others the present,
to him had been given tomorrow:
he alone who saw a three-legged toad
scuttle under a rock,
a tunny-fish in the tide with miniscule arms,
sadness in a turtle shell . . .

                *   *   *   *

I saw his name in the check-out line again today—
among headlines of the end-times;
reminded again of his clarity,
still describing his vision
to an old-fashioned world.
It was raining outside,
the petals of the dogwoods were washed by the rain—
I saw him in his cell on the island,
listening to the fluting of the wind,
one candle for friendship

and egg-shells on the table,
writing down everything in his own careful words.

If the foreheads of our parents bore the signs of the elect,
who were we to have stared
in their faces and known,
who had to learn from them
how to see even ourselves?
Perhaps it explains everything
in a reverse sort of way:
that the fault was in us, not them—
to be expected, you might say, when faith ends.

Part Two

Frankfurt

There was no damage to the house—
except the mirror was shattered,
there in the hall—the blast
left a crater the size of a cow in the yard—
It had a star of Bethlehem crack,
creating a kaleidoscope
in plain color
of the light in the hall
and whoever entered,
doubly fractured in the panes of the door . . .

The owner didn't want Americans here,
wouldn't fix a thing—
removed all the wainscoting from the library
and stored it in the garage.
If they didn't like it they could complain
to the Occupation Authority—
Let *them* fix the mirror
if it mattered that much;
which it didn't of course, so it stayed,
broken like a pair of spectacles
crushed on a road.

The stairway was like a ladder at the end
of the hall—
rooms cold and dark,
ceilings too high to be warm;
bedrooms silent and cold . . .

where sleep, when it came,
seemed to come from without,
from voices in another room,
a moth at the screen,
the click of a stylus
no one removes . . .

and from the sleep of other children
who once used these rooms
for a different kind of sleep,
a babe in a basket
on the wall above their beds,
guarded by an ibis
among African rushes—

Did they feel, before the first bombs,
the dark of that tide
rising on a distant coast,
to reach those lights
that would not sink to voluntary ends—?

Or did a drooping hand
finally turn a blank page
and look out, as children sometimes do,
and see a leaf drop
or a sparrow land, legs up,
in a gust of wind?

—Or were their blinds
already pulled on parades,
bonfires and night-marches,

on an intolerance of frailties,
by careful hands?

The crawl-spaces under the hedges were still.
The Isar slid like a slow snake
along its pebbled shore.
A fish-pond was there,
an eye with a clouded lens.
A mist seemed to hang over the grounds,
lingering in the sand-box
and over the swings,
when the sun was slow to rise . . .

And two children crouched,
hiding under bushes . . .
They had taken shelter there,
though there was no danger—
as though it had come to them
suddenly, the way things come
of a sudden to sparrows
that vanish on a notion,
leaving their crumbs unclaimed—

In the lawn behind the house, a door,
an open stairway:
Luftschutzbunker they called it . . .
I counted the steps,
as if I would need to know
their number to return:
at the bottom
a turn brought you darkness—

a place
only the blind could enter.

While the world remained locked
against itself,
the earth beneath the storm
was at peace—
Tracked vehicles left no print.
The hair of mothers mingled
with the hair of their children;
old men out of their slippers
were no longer cold,
and their sons embraced the earth
they could no longer protect,
and all were at rest . . .

*   *   *   *

What if something happened to your eyes while you slept?
What if you woke in the morning
and everything looked different?
What if it was like a lever had been pulled
and the world that had seemed
normal was now suddenly in focus?
What if you were the only one who saw it,
because no one else noticed, no one
said anything?

—What if it didn't even happen at night
but maybe between the swing and the sandbox
or while running home for dinner
or going out to play
or even getting ready for bed,
you suddenly looked up
and a clock forgot to tick and *there*,
things became real—
The world turned into a medieval woodcut . . .

This was what happened here.
This happened to me.
Where I was when it happened
or what I was doing
or if it even happened all at once—
or like a pair of shoes you outgrow,
it happened over time, I don't know.
What I remember is this:

when people spoke,
scrolls came out of their mouths,
words were that clear.
Certain moments had borders
of tendrils and birds
to make sure you got the point.
No more shades of indeterminate grays:
things were black and white
to the point of transparency.

Colors were for fairy-tales.
When color disappeared,
you knew you were awake.

The world was like a saw blade
on a workbench of a parent,
a drill-bit or a chisel,
a thing you could get cut with.

So I stood again at the fish-pond
and looked at it really—
its water full of cattails,
its walkway cracked,
cross-hatched with grass,
each leaf in its circumambient
hedge like a twig in a weir.

Here I had set a toy loose
in its soup of dead life,
and had watched its slow fall
to a tangle of lily-pads
where it lay still,
capsized, its voyage ended . . .

This was the power:
The pond, more than a pond,
a shattered tree in the park,
more than a tree,
a stairwell in a house,
closed off and unused,
where the silent and the empty
crack the taut nerve—
more than a stairwell.

This was the place we were directed to return to,
to the brook and the tea-cup
hidden in a tree trunk
with a spell to protect them—
To take a drink from the brook
and remember the spell,
and be whole again beyond confusion . . .

No more was I like some misshapen thing
with overgrown eyes,
afraid of being seen without seeing,
hiding in the corners of significant scenes.
The spell had been turned on its head.
Still I see the world as a transfigured place.
Still I see through it—
though I cannot see beyond it.

A last memory of a dream:
the young consular officer and his wife,
staring up at a cross,
hands shaped for shadow-puppets.
Above them, as if held up on forks,
bodies writhe, being lifted
to the sky—
Blood sprays like a fountain
and a loincloth unfurls . . .
though whether I dreamed this then
or last night, I can't tell.

Part Three

Home Leave

I have a large room with wide shelves about the walls.
The shelves are filled with toys.
Sometimes children come in
and they look at the floor,
so big and so bare,
and they pick up a broom
and pay homage to the floor—
so polished and shiny,
made of lodge pole pine
from the slopes of the Rockies
and imported hardwoods
from the forests of Germany . . .
I too love a bright floor—
When the children are gone
and the office is closed
I too sweep the floor,
I—a pediatric psychiatrist,
I put the toys back on the shelves.
I set its clear shine free
from the clutter of lives.
I go home then, satisfied.

But there are some that don't care for the floor
and love only the shelves;
they will spend hours arranging its toys,
lining up the palominos,
setting the spinning-tops
next to the dump-trucks,

tidying up the tea-cups—
or some that don't want to touch toys at all . . .
They will go all around
and lie down when they're done.
These I don't understand.

Now it is silent.
The sun sets in the playroom.
The light of a winter afternoon
congeals in its floor . . .
Women still wear their pre-war coats;
nylons are in short supply.
You would not know peace had returned
except for an abundance of perambulators
under the war-weary sky.

These are my patients,
the first-fruits of peace:
stutterers and echo-talkers,
some who had developed normally
until a certain Sunday
when the world burst into rhyme . . .
those who won't speak at all—
and those who can't hear,
though nothing is wrong with their ears.

This is what they tell me:
the world everywhere is the same.
Every city is the same.
Every track along a river, the same.
Every street is named Market
or a number or a point of the compass

or a vanishing tribe—
and every crowd is the same.

The flame in their eyes
is hard-edged and crystal
and in the eyes of some
the light could cut stone,
and in the eyes of the race-man
the flame is a smudge-pot—

In the dark of the Bijou
where children come with their nickels
and weary couples come
to get out of the heat,
as if on a single iris
images shimmer and swim—

Swinging doors close on the visions
to keep them inside;
let the sleepers relish their dreams.
The lobby prepares you
for your carpet ride,
its concession stand like
a juke-box of candy.
The children are wise to me,
and I am wise to the children.

Listen—yesterday in the park
while leaving the path,
I knocked against a rock—
and saw white worms writhe

in sudden recognition . . . .
so beautiful in the dark,
so repulsive to sight.

It had rained hard the night before,
whole limbs crashed down.
After great storms
sometimes a certain stillness begins.

Meanwhile, shadows wane . . .
See how they shrink
against the storefronts on a summer morning,
—where even normals
seek to flee the sun's glare,
and find no shade.

I fear the paralysis that comes in the night—
the varnish of sleep
that refuses to break . . .
the world pressing around you,
and you, awake,
unable to move,
buried in your own body . . . .

Is this no waking terror then,
but a only nightmare—
a dream of waking,
whose meaning is this:
to remain forever asleep
and never wake up?

I take it for a wonder.
I write it down in my notes,
a thing to be pondered—

Here is a list of the illnesses I have treated:
abominations of the body,
physical deformities,
blemishes of character
and weak wills—

domineering and unnatural passions,
treacherous or rigid beliefs,
a record of mental disorders,
imprisonment, addiction,
alcoholism, unemployment—

suicidal attempts,
radical political behaviors,
Jehovah's Witnesses,
gypsies, stigmas of race,
race defilers—
The rest I have pitied.

That was the year a man fractured my jaw
and shoved me in a urinal.
I awake and walk alone through my rooms,
my head full of vestibules.
The ground recoils,
the earth gives up its dead.

   * * * *

Now the sun sets . . .
Wide streets are empty under the winter sky;
people drive as if gasoline was still rationed.
Women lock their babies inside
to go to the store;
help is in short-supply.

The floor is swept again;
the toys are set in orderly shadows.
Houses crouch under mountains.
The streets of this development
were laid out in a grid,
milk-bottles on back steps.

As if this were the last day
of all days that have passed,
the afternoon takes its own time to end.
A last light lingers
on a soldier and his bride,

there—on the mantel,
standing at attention
in an overcast frame.
Thoughts take refuge
among the mundane:
a pair of red pumps,
cuba libras and a murder mystery . . .
But the pattern breaks,
as it always seems to,
on an abandoned lemonade.

What is this thing
that is collapsing around them?
A woman with a stroller
stops to smooth a victory roll
in the window of a store.
The secret she learns
is to control what she looks at,
to look at herself—or nothing at all.

They will not find what they seek,
these soldiers and their brides.
Somewhere under a glacier
of incendiaries an idea died.
A dead god takes his ideas to himself,
rolls up their words like a scroll.

The last light that falls
finds them already smaller,
fading behind the reflection
they have already become,
nothing but a smudge . . .

Part Four

Germantown

Something is wrong in this place.
This is a suburb and things are too perfect.
Boulevards are as empty as tundra.
Houses are as small as the eyelids of dolls.
Something is approaching my heart
like a snake on the branch of a tree . . .

From the side of a road,
cars pass with speed-tails like comets.
It is like an exhibit in the hall
of an American museum,
everyday life in the ordinary world.
I search for a word to describe it—

I have heard there are people who are stereo-blind,
they see no dimensions at all.
Say instead then that I am stereo-*hyper* . . .

Objects exist in exaggerated planes.
People stand out against
backgrounds they no longer belong to.
Surfaces are flat and spaces are stretched.
Everywhere I turn, objects are popping
up out of their frames.
I am in a world that is over-dimensional.
I am in the pages of a pop-up book.

Perhaps I have stayed in this suburb too long.
Perhaps like my neighbors
I fell asleep in this place.
Perhaps I have been lulled
by the conformity of traffic.

Years pass like the wave
of crow-wings, too wide to hurry,
children grown, yourself tracing
the lines of a frown;
here you drive for hours
without remembering a light,
you take a series of buses and trains
without missing a stop . . .

Rain-bead curtains are gray on the hills,
on the small-scale valleys and fields,
on the ghosts-forms of barns.
Worms flush out in spring rains,
cicada wings wash down in gutters.
Open-House signs blossom
and the rain washes children's
chalk from the sidewalks.

The young wife watches children play;
they play adjacent to each other
but they don't play together.
The young wife wonders
why her husband isn't happy.

The town center is a stage-set.
It was built entirely from memory—
though I don't believe it ever existed.
Its house-fronts are brick,
a brick walk runs along the one block
of Main Street,
two if you count the parking-lot—

Potemkin-people sit out on the sidewalk,
at tables and chairs
that are chained to each other.
The air is always full of exhaust.
At the Dutch market,
a gull and a coal-scuttle bonnet,
skate-boarders steering
between pharaonic beards.

For those who need instructions to the good life,
everything is laid out
like a map in real space—
There is your parking-place
and beyond it the highway.
Husbands and wives go in different directions,
children in another . . .

An old woman in a pashmina,
wandering alone among the houses,
lays claim to the silence
after the last car has gone,
the last middle-schooler gone,
the last school-bus departed . . .

I will not disturb your peace, old woman.
We are both foreigners here.
This world looks no more real
to me than it does to you.
You are in a strange land,
and it appears I can not wake up in any land . . .

As when lights dim in a theater
and images stab out of the screen
when your eyes are expecting flatness,
so gulls in a parking-lot,
scrapping over a Happy Meal,
are cut-outs against asphalt,
so a constellation of traffic-lights
glow at the end of their beams.

It is raining and the rain parts like sheers;
wipers clarify its imprecision.
A gentle rhythm sets in.
Intersections fold into place like origami.
House fronts unfold,
doll-roofs unfold under low clouds.

If I could have believed in the world of Forms,
life would have been a tolerable
reflection of itself.
I could have lived like a cormorant
on the mirror of the shore—

But existence is a room and there is only
one exit—
but that exit is only a closet
with a burned-out light . . .

The children are comfortable here.
They stay indoors all day,
they never go out anyway.
For a while their video games amuse them.
When they get bored
the walls become trampolines.
Dads try to take them out
and are accused of abuse.

When I go out, there is no outdoors at all,
only a bigger indoors.
It has a roof and as many walls
as there are images around me:
a Do Not Feed the Ducks sign,
lit in a spotlight
that ignites from within,
a young maple,
its trunk wrapped in beaver-mesh,
is a scoop of pistachio . . .

Take a pop-up book and open it's pages.
It's a pop-up world that unfolds
like the wings of a dragonfly.
But though this world
looks more real than the page,
it is a crude kind of reality;
it is an artificial reality—

Houses, trees and power-lines
all are separate from each other—
and you too, in this new kind of world,
are a pop-up on the page,
separate from the page,
separate from the universe—

It seems the skin has been
peeled off the world,
and I wonder, how did it happen?
Someone has skinned
the reality from the world,
and I am seeing it raw.

I keep my mind on my chores,
try to keep up-to-date with my to-dos.
Only in the car on the long drive
home, or when I take the dog
on his morning patrol,
or on his long darkening patrol . . .

I have been told I should watch more TV.

Instead I am here, on an overpass
above the Interstate.
I'm looking through a scrim of rain
across a series of stage-flats . . .
A mountain humps in the west,
rising like the fin
of a dolphin from a forested sea.

I snap the rubber-band
I wear on my wrist,
hard against the veins.

*   *   *   *

People go down in the basements of churches,
in the basements of libraries,
in community meeting rooms;
they go down back-stairs,
take exits into obscure stairwells,
glimpse gray tires through ground-level windows,
last year's leaves under dim grates;
chairs are taken from stacks
and tables pushed against walls.
The air smells of toilet-stalls and old carpets.
Cold cups of coffee are poured, if any
is left—

We are underground and in the backrooms
of buildings.
We are out of sight of the houses,
the ribbon-cut roads and the well-ordered
landscapes.
We find time in the corners of our lives,
in the evenings after work,
between homework and dinner,
in the remnants of weekends,
between soccer and gymnastics.

We are the people
coming out of convenience stores
as though with invisible crutches,
who seem as though missing an arm
or a leg though no matter how often
you count, they add up
to the right number,
or who speak with an impediment
though no one asks us to repeat ourselves,

a woman who has had five husbands
and the one she has now is not her own,
a man who knows personally
that strong drink is raging
and wine is a mocker—
The betrayed and the betrayers,
the abused and the abusers.
We pull our chairs in a ring,
—and a silence begins.

Somehow in this silence a healing occurs.
It takes courage to break the silence
and speak.
Call it the Age of Recovery—
recovery from adverse childhood
experiences,
from abuse and co-dependence,
from frightening parental behaviors,
from uncertainty and self-doubt,
from things that didn't happen
in this country,
and a few things that did . . .

And maybe some things that didn't happen to you individually
but happened to humanity,
because we're all part of humanity,
because humanity is consciousness
and consciousness is One—

And a woman will go home tonight
and write on Facebook ten thousand times
I deserve to be loved,
and someone else will write
if you have to make laws that hurt people
to prove you're religious and moral
you have no religion
and you are not moral—

And somewhere a man
will go home again tonight
and try to stop smoking
again,
and fail . . .

Part Five

Epilogue

I stepped out of the check-out line
and went out across the parking-lot under the dogwoods,
and felt the rain startle me,
and made a fearless moral inventory
of everything in me.

Still I am surrounded by Christians—
They get up in the morning
and walk their dogs and go running
and wait for buses and hail cabs
and clutch cups of coffee and tea,
and do the same when it's raining,
as if the weather were between us
on an invisible pane—

But what matters is that the sky burns
like a crocus in the morning
and birds sing in bushes
and the newspaper comes
and centuries of overcast astonishingly lift,
and a koi seems to float
through the morning commute,
and windshields give their glass to its scales . . .

"The old gods ate ambrosia—
but the saints are our gods;
they dined on olive-oil and bread,
wine and a little salt;

sometimes they grew organs
on the outside of their bodies.
Why should we now be called pagans
because our God has three heads
and impregnated a woman?
The new christians
inveigh against us,
denounce the unreason of faith,
the insanity of miracles;
shake their heads at our stubbornness . . . "

Again the old church, renovated by mortars,
its cracked forms collecting
dust under fallen vaults,
with their tongs and pulleys,
their vials of dried blood—
Do they still answer the question,
what will happen to me?
A bearded man raises
a hand as if offended,
offering his gesture with a finger blown off.

Time to clean house—take down
the unremoved card on the Christmas doorframe:
a man in a hill town,
the air around his head like a candle,
while columnar bodies
surround him in a peristyle,
their names unfurling on gilded scrolls;
a widow and seven brothers
on a hill in the background,

still confounding salvation.
In resurrectione, cuius de his erit uxor?

Inside, angel singers fill the page—
their haloes like bubbles
in a flute of champagne,
massing their orisons
on the tongues of hummingbirds.

We can only be so close
to each other;
always something saves us.
Yet still we struggle
for the perfect word,
the faithful gesture,
the one true inflection
that keeps the leaf balanced
on the edge of the bough.

*   *   *   *

Today I found a leaf.
It had been burned through by the sun,
leaving only its veins.
I turned it over in my hand,
lightly touching its fragility.
Its season is over . . .
only its connections remain.

BIOGRAPHICAL NOTE

Biographical Note

George Churchill and Nancy Goss were married in 1944. After the war, Lieutenant Churchill joined the Foreign Service. With two children in tow, including the author, the family was first sent to Germany where they lived in Frankfort for a year, then in Munich. This was in 1950. Another child was born there; eventually George and Nancy would have two more, one born in Rome and the youngest in Turkey. An additional post included Singapore. After Turkey the family returned to the States.